CGP

KS2 English
SAT Buster

Answer Book
Poetry · Fiction · Non-Fiction

New!

Fiction

Fiction

> **N.B. An 'E.g.' before an answer
> means that it's just a suggestion.**
>
> *For questions which ask for an <u>opinion</u>, <u>interpretation</u> or <u>explanation</u>,
> there <u>won't</u> always be one 'correct' answer. Pupils' answers to these
> questions may <u>vary</u> from the answers we've suggested, but they should
> give a similar amount of <u>detail</u>, and should always be <u>based on the text</u>.*

The Baking Battle

Pages 6-7 — Fact Retrieval Questions

1. **1 mark**
    Jack: small OR skinny
    AND 1 mark
    Demi: has a ponytail

2. **1 mark**
    quickly

3. **1 mark**
    They knocked over the bag of flour.

4. **1 mark**
    Demi helped Jack lift the bag of flour up to the scales.

5. **1 mark**
    30 minutes

6. **1 mark for any of the following answers**
    weighing out ingredients precisely
    greasing the cake tin

7. **1 mark**
    Demi and Jack

8. **1 mark**
    They are gold.
    AND 1 mark
    They have the image of a chef's hat on the front.

9. **1 mark**
    E.g. They ate it.

10. **1 mark for all correct**
    whisked the batter — just Jack
    tidied up the table — Demi and Jack
    won the competition — Alison and Tyrone

Pages 8-9 — Inference Questions

1. **1 mark**
    E.g. They felt unhappy about it.

2. **1 mark**
    opinion

3. **a) 1 mark**
    competitive
    b) 1 mark
    bossy

4. **1 mark**
    grumbling under her breath

5. **1 mark for any of the following answers**
    the frown slipped from her face
    she smiled broadly

6. **1 mark**
    They glanced at each other urgently.

7. **1 mark**
    E.g. They felt happy.
    OR 2 marks
    E.g. I think they felt happy, because it says they ate their cake enthusiastically.

8. **1 mark each for any of the following answers
    2 marks in total**
    They split the tasks according to what they were good at.
    They helped each other with the tasks they weren't good at.
    They put aside their differences to work together.
    They completed their cake on time.

Page 10 — Word Meaning Questions

1. **1 mark**
    looked

2. **1 mark**
    fragments

3. **1 mark**
    lifted

4. **1 mark**
    E.g. gripping

Page 11 — Summary Questions

1. **1 mark**
    Demi and Jack's cake-making starts off badly.

2. **1 mark**
    It's better to work together.

Page 11 — Structure Question

1. **1 mark**
    From that point on, they stopped trying to fight against each other.

An Underground City

Pages 16-17 — Fact Retrieval Questions

1. **1 mark**
    the lobby

2. **1 mark**
    They got stuck in traffic.

3. **1 mark**
    looking at some photos

4. **1 mark**
    There was a strong, earthy smell.

5. **1 mark for any of the following answers**
    bunk beds
    striped bedding
    odd bits of furniture

6. **1 mark**
    The air-raid shelters were used to escape bombing.

7. **1 mark**
    post office — letters
    AND 1 mark
    kitchen — pots and pans

8. **1 mark**
    Tia

9. **1 mark**
    E.g They needed to find information for their homework project.
    OR 2 marks
    E.g. They couldn't find enough information for their homework project elsewhere, and they thought the museum might have the information they needed.

Fiction

Pages 18-19 — Inference Questions

1. **1 mark**
   E.g. They felt like they had been stuck in traffic for years.

2. **1 mark**
   stretched away into the darkness

3. **1 mark for any of the following answers**
   It says the room was cramped.
   It says it was like a prison cell.
   It says it was "crowded".

4. **a) 1 mark**
   exciting
   b) 1 mark
   E.g. You can tell this because he grinned as he imagined sleeping in the shelters.

5. **1 mark**
   E.g. They have lots of different things you find on a city street, such as a post office.

6. **1 mark**
   E.g. He thought they would have to sleep on them.

7. **1 mark**
   E.g. She felt angry.
   OR 2 marks
   E.g. She felt angry. You can tell this because she frowned.

8. **1 mark**
   the ink poured out of their pens

9. **1 mark for one correct**
   2 marks for all correct
   Nathan sees the door to the tunnels. — excitement
   Nathan enters the tunnels. — amazement
   Nathan realises they are lost. — fear

Page 20 — Word Meaning Questions

1. **1 mark**
   ajar

2. **1 mark**
   fascinated

3. **1 mark**
   E.g. stopped still

4. **1 mark**
   anxious

5. **1 mark**
   keen

Page 21 — Summary Questions

1. **1 mark**
   Exploring the shelters

2. **1 mark**
   Panicking about being lost

Page 21 — Prediction Question

1. **1 mark**
   E.g. Yes, because they found it exciting at first.
   OR 2 marks
   E.g. No, because they got lost and it was scary. Amanda also told them the tunnels are dangerous, so now they know it would be a bad idea.

The Old Photogra

Pages 26-27 — Fact Re

1. **1 mark**
   watch Jackson's favourite film

2. **a) 1 mark**
   It was a good opportunity for some father-son bonding.
   b) 1 mark
   E.g. He likes tidiness.

3. **1 mark**
   morning

4. **1 mark**
   E.g. His dad went to get them both a drink.

5. **1 mark for both correct**
   some puzzle games
   a piggy bank

6. **1 mark each for any of the following answers**
   2 marks in total
   He looks like he's in his mid-twenties.
   His face is unlined.
   His face has a youthful glow.
   He is wearing a turquoise suit.
   He is wearing a sequinned suit.

7. **1 mark**
   all over Europe

8. **1 mark**
   They found travelling tiring.

9. **1 mark**
   She laughed with surprise.

10. **1 mark**
    Seeing: the delight on the spectators' faces
    AND 1 mark
    Hearing: the roar of the crowd

Pages 28-29 — Inference Questions

1. **1 mark**
   He was satisfied with it.

2. **1 mark**
   E.g. He didn't like being asked.

3. **1 mark**
   Everything was dusty.

4. **1 mark**
   the audience

5. **1 mark for any of the following answers**
   They are in a poor state.
   They are cracked.
   The paper is faded.
   The paper is peeling away.

6. **1 mark**
   twirled one around with ease

7. **1 mark each for any of the following answers**
   2 marks in total
   It says they threw the juggling clubs quickly.
   It says their hands moved quickly.
   It says they used complex combinations.

8. **1 mark**
   E.g. It was surprising because he hadn't known his parents used to be jugglers.
   AND 1 mark
   E.g. It was inspiring because it made him want to do juggling tricks like his parents.

Fiction

Page 30 — Word Meaning Questions

1. **1 mark**
complicated

2. **1 mark**
E.g. it's large

3. **1 mark**
darted

4. **1 mark**
ugly

5. **1 mark**
pleaded

Page 31 — Summary Questions

1. **1 mark for all correct**
Jackson's dad likes things to be tidy. — 2
Jackson and his dad tidy the garage together. — 3
Jackson examines the old photograph closely. — 5
Jackson tidies alone, then finds a piece of card. — 4

2. **1 mark**
People can have hidden and interesting pasts.

Page 31 — Comparison Question

1. **1 mark**
E.g. At first he thinks it is dull, but later he becomes more enthusiastic.

A Visit to Baba Yaga

Pages 36-37 — Fact Retrieval Questions

1. **1 mark**
two weeks

2. **1 mark**
a needle

3. **1 mark**
iron

4. **1 mark**
bread
AND 1 mark
ham

5. **1 mark**
It was squeaking.

6. **1 mark**
It's twisted.
AND 1 mark
There is smoke coming out of it.

7. **1 mark**
quietly

8. **1 mark**
weaving

9. **1 mark**
in a corner

10. **1 mark**
It kept the loom going so Baba Yaga didn't realise that Natasha had left.

11. **1 mark for any of the following answers**
Natasha had given it food to eat.
Natasha was nicer to it than Baba Yaga was.

Pages 38-39 — Inference Questions

1. **1 mark**
(wild and) wicked wood

2. **1 mark each for any of the following answers**
2 marks in total
She was tyrannical.
She made Natasha's life a misery.
She made Natasha do chores all day.
She never said thank you.

3. **a) 1 mark**
E.g. fear
b) 1 mark
E.g. She was afraid of being eaten by Baba Yaga.

4. **1 mark**
E.g. She had realised that it was not Natasha who was speaking to her.

5. **1 mark each for any of the following answers**
2 marks in total
She let out a deafening shriek.
She called it a flea-infested traitor.
She gave it a poisonous glare.

6. **a) 1 mark**
caring
b) 1 mark
E.g. She looked after the animals and the gate.
OR 2 marks
E.g. She gave food to the animals and kept none for herself.
She oiled the gate to stop it squeaking.

7. **1 mark**
E.g. Because he was sad.
OR 2 marks
E.g. He was sad because Natasha was nearly eaten by Baba Yaga, and because his wife tried to kill his daughter.

Page 40 — Word Meaning Questions

1. **1 mark**
E.g. unlucky

2. **1 mark**
pleased

3. **1 mark**
threatening

4. **1 mark**
E.g. quickly

5. **1 mark**
slender

Page 41 — Summary Question

1. **a) 1 mark**
Baba Yaga is cruel.
b) 1 mark
E.g. Baba Yaga tried to eat Natasha.
OR 2 marks
E.g. Baba Yaga treated the dog, cat and gate cruelly by not feeding or looking after them, and she is known to eat children.

Page 41 — Language Question

1. **1 mark**
E.g. To show how hungry the dog was.

Non-Fiction

Non-Fiction

> **N.B.** An 'E.g.' before an answer
> means that it's just a suggestion.
>
> *For questions which ask for an <u>opinion</u>, <u>interpretation</u> or <u>explanation</u>, there <u>won't</u> always be one 'correct' answer. Pupils' answers to these questions may <u>vary</u> from the answers we've suggested, but they should give a similar amount of <u>detail</u>, and should always be <u>based on the text</u>.*

Dare to Dance!

Pages 6-7 — Fact Retrieval Questions

1. **1 mark**
   easy to learn

2. **1 mark each for any of the following answers**
   2 marks in total
   It's rewarding.
   It's fun.
   So that they can learn spectacular skills.
   So that they can show off to their friends.

3. **1 mark for any of the following answers**
   It gets the heart pumping.
   It helps build muscle.
   It helps you improve your flexibility.

4. **1 mark for any of the following answers**
   The sort of music you like.
   Whether you want to dance with a partner or on your own.

5. **1 mark**
   It can help you pick up other forms of dance.

6. **1 mark**
   It's often performed in music videos.

7. **1 mark**
   doing moves near to the ground

8. **1 mark**
   samba
   AND 1 mark
   salsa

9. **1 mark**
   his best friend

10. **1 mark**
    He is giving his first performance soon.

Pages 8-9 — Inference Questions

1. **1 mark**
   E.g. They might avoid dancing if they think they have two left feet.

2. **1 mark**
   If the first style they try doesn't suit them.

3. **1 mark each for any of the following answers**
   2 marks in total
   They train as hard as athletes.
   They perform impressive leaps.
   They do high-flying lifts.
   They make difficult moves look effortless.

4. **1 mark**
   not to be tried at home

5. **1 mark**
   They are very popular.

6. **1 mark for all correct**
   There are lots of different dance styles. — Fact
   Ballet dancers are impressive to watch. — Opinion
   'Locking' involves freezing in position between moves. — Fact
   Ballroom and Latin dancing belong in the past. — Opinion

7. **1 mark**
   He had to be dragged along by his friend.

8. **1 mark**
   Because he plays the drums, he has a good sense of rhythm, which is important for tap dancing.
   AND 1 mark
   He likes making different sounds on the floor with his shoes as it's a bit like playing drums.

9. **1 mark**
   E.g. They enjoy dancing so much that they don't want to stop.

Page 10 — Word Meaning Questions

1. **1 mark**
   impressive

2. **1 mark**
   forget about

3. **1 mark**
   think about

4. **1 mark**
   series

Page 11 — Summary Questions

1. **1 mark**
   people's reasons for dancing

2. **1 mark**
   everyone should try dancing

Page 11 — Structure Questions

1. **1 mark for all correct**
   How to choose a dance style — 2
   Someone's experience of dancing — 4
   Different dance types — 3

2. **1 mark**
   E.g. It talks about finding the dance style that's "right for you", which is also mentioned in the introduction.

Drive-in to 1950s America

Pages 16-17 — Fact Retrieval Questions

1. **1 mark each for any of the following answers**
   3 marks in total
   colourful diners with black-and-white checked floors
   polka dot dresses
   leather jackets

2. **1 mark**
   They needed a babysitter if they wanted to see a film in the evening.

3. **1 mark for any of the following answers**
   So that the cars in each row were at different heights.
   So that everyone had a clear view of the screen.

Non-Fiction

4. 1 mark
1933

5. 1 mark
around 400

6. 1 mark each for any of the following answers
2 marks in total
Speaker-posts were placed near each car.
Speakers were hung on cars' wing mirrors.
The sound was played through people's car radios.

7. 1 mark
night

8. 1 mark for both correct
They couldn't show many films each day.
Bad weather put people off attending.

9. 1 mark
1930s-1960s

10. 1 mark
the USA

Pages 18-19 — Inference Questions

1. 1 mark
exciting

2. 1 mark
an opinion

3. 1 mark
They gave a lot of time and money to them.

4. 1 mark
E.g. It made drive-in cinemas less popular.
OR 2 marks
E.g. Technology made drive-in cinemas less popular, because people were able to watch films at home.

5. 1 mark
In the twenty-first century, drive-in cinemas continue to face an uphill battle.

6. 1 mark
The weather is often bad.

7. 1 mark
E.g. It makes them feel excited.
OR 2 marks
E.g. It makes them feel excited because it suggests that going to a drive-in cinema would easily take them to a different time and a different part of the world.

Page 20 — Word Meaning Questions

1. 1 mark
distracting

2. 1 mark
E.g. observed

3. 1 mark
answer

4. 1 mark
attractive

Page 21 — Summary Questions

1. 1 mark
How drive-in cinemas developed

2. 1 mark
Drive-in cinemas had money issues.

Page 21 — Language Question

1. 1 mark
E.g. To show that drive-in cinemas had no control over the weather and that it could have a really bad effect on them.

Inside the World of Jam

Pages 26-27 — Fact Retrieval Questions

1. 1 mark
reporter

2. a) 1 mark
(two slices of) toast
b) 1 mark
scones
AND 1 mark
Victoria sponge

3. 1 mark each for any of the following answers
2 marks in total
the UK
Germany
Switzerland

4. 1 mark for all correct
Robert Jacobs makes jam all year round. — False
Robert makes his jam at home. — True
Robert uses old family recipes to make his jam. — True
Robert has never changed the recipes he uses. — False

5. 1 mark
strawberry

6. 1 mark
tomato ketchup

7. 1 mark
3 years

8. 1 mark
Because her children were bored with the spreads from the supermarket.

9. 1 mark
patience
AND 1 mark
a working fire alarm

Pages 28-29 — Inference Questions

1. 1 mark
E.g. He loves jam and wants to learn more about it.

2. 1 mark
E.g. He won't reduce the amount of time, care and attention he puts into his jams just to make more money.

3. 1 mark
E.g. He won't tell Benjamin Dejar what he puts in his jam to make it so delicious.

4. 1 mark
E.g. He finds it hard not to eat the whole jar.

5. 1 mark
E.g. They often appear on people's breakfast tables.

6. 1 mark for all correct
Lara Fontesca lives in Manchester. — Fact
Lara makes more than one flavour of jam. — Fact
Lara's tastiest jam is apple and cinnamon flavour. — Opinion
Supermarket jam flavours are boring. — Opinion

7. 1 mark
E.g. She seems inventive.
OR 2 marks
E.g. She seems imaginative, because she says that she enjoys using her imagination to come up with new flavours of jam.
OR 3 marks
E.g. She seems creative, because she comes up with unusual jam flavours like "tomato ketchup". She also seems determined, because she says she was never tempted to give up, even though setting up her business was a "huge challenge".

8. 1 mark
He grimaced in dismay.

9. 1 mark
E.g. He thinks they taste nice.
OR 2 marks
E.g. He really likes them. He says that they are "nothing short of spectacular".

Page 30 — Word Meaning Questions

1. 1 mark
E.g. thinking about

2. 1 mark
transform

3. 1 mark
E.g. satisfying

4. 1 mark
pausing

Page 31 — Summary Questions

1. 1 mark
It tells you about a jam company in Cheshire.

2. 1 mark
It's possible to experiment with jam flavours.

Page 31 — Comparison Question

1. 1 mark
E.g. Robert Jacobs makes traditional flavours, but Lara Fontesca makes unusual flavours.
OR 2 marks
E.g. Robert Jacobs's jams use traditional, "well-recognised" flavours like strawberry and raspberry. Lara Fontesca uses "outlandish" flavours, such as "bacon sandwich" flavour.

The Great Wall of China

Pages 36-37 — Fact Retrieval Questions

1. 1 mark for any of the following answers
countryside
desert
mountains

2. 1 mark for any of the following answers
a powerful telescope
a powerful camera

3. 1 mark
more than 13,000 miles

4. 1 mark
to protect the country against invasion from the north
AND 1 mark
to safeguard the Silk Road

5. 1 mark for any of the following answers
luxury foods
precious stones
fabrics
silk

6. 1 mark
(December) 1987

7. 1 mark
Cable cars have been put up.

8. 1 mark for both correct
There are many towers along the Great Wall.
Soldiers helped to build the Great Wall.

9. 1 mark each for any of the following answers
3 marks in total
Visitors have left litter.
Visitors have drawn graffiti.
Some parts have been destroyed to make roads.
Erosion has caused chunks to crumble away.

Pages 38-39 — Inference Questions

1. 1 mark
one of the world's most recognisable sights

2. 1 mark
stating a fact

3. 1 mark
Visitors can walk where soldiers did.

4. 1 mark
a widespread myth

5. 1 mark
E.g. They occur naturally rather than being built by people.
AND 1 mark
E.g. They are difficult to get past so they would help stop the invaders.

6. 1 mark
E.g. The text says the work was exhausting.
OR 2 marks
E.g. Workers had to "painstakingly" carry heavy materials up to the wall on their backs and shoulders. The text says that this was "exhausting work", which killed many people.

7. 1 mark for any of the following answers
The story is described as a "legend".
The text says that the story is a "rumour".

8. 1 mark
E.g. It is the longest man-made structure on Earth.
OR 2 marks
E.g. The wall is the longest man-made structure in the world, which makes it an "enormous feat of human engineering". It is also important because it records a lot of Chinese history.
OR 3 marks
E.g. The wall is especially valuable to humans as it is the longest man-made structure. It is also "one of the world's most recognisable sights". Because the wall is so old, it can help "bring memories of China's distant past to life", which means that people can learn a lot about history from the wall.

Non-Fiction / Poetry

9. 1 mark
E.g. The writer feels shocked that people would damage the wall.
OR 2 marks
E.g. The writer feels angry and upset about it. They say that the damage is "shocking" and that it spoils the wall's "historic beauty".

Page 40 — Word Meaning Questions

1. 1 mark
cautious

2. 1 mark
immense

3. 1 mark
disintegrate

4. 1 mark
leading

Page 41 — Summary Question

1. a) 1 mark
There are myths about the Great Wall.
b) 1 mark
E.g. The paragraphs describe things people believe about the wall which aren't true, for example that it can be seen from the moon.

Page 41 — Prediction Question

1. 1 mark
E.g. No, because it faces lots of threats like erosion and graffiti.
OR 2 marks
E.g. Yes, because the Chinese government began a "mission" to rebuild the wall, which shows that they want to protect it. It is also a UNESCO World Heritage Site, and I think this will help to protect it for future generations.
OR 3 marks
E.g. No, because it is in danger from erosion, which has already made some parts "crumble". It is also threatened by human actions such as people destroying parts of it to make way for roads. The fact that the wall is so long makes it even harder to protect, because it takes a lot of work to look after it.

Poetry

> **N.B. An 'E.g.' before an answer means that it's just a suggestion.**
> *For questions which ask for an opinion, interpretation or explanation, there won't always be one 'correct' answer. Pupils' answers to these questions may vary from the answers we've suggested, but they should give a similar amount of detail, and should always be based on the text.*

Lost Dog

Page 4 — Fact Retrieval Questions

1. 1 mark for any of the following answers
"each new tread"
footsteps

2. 1 mark
does not bark

3. 1 mark each for any of the following answers
2 marks in total
lifting one paw
cocking an ear
staying in the same place

4. 1 mark
It comes from down the street.

5. 1 mark
trembles

Page 5 — Inference Questions

1. 1 mark
eyes

2. 1 mark
excited

3. 1 mark
E.g. He loves the person a lot.

4. 1 mark each for any of the following answers
2 marks in total
He doesn't bark.
He doesn't move even though he wants to.
He only moves when he is called.

Page 6 — Word Meaning Questions

1. 1 mark
wishful

2. 1 mark
His feet are moving.

3. 1 mark
E.g. trying hard

4. 1 mark
E.g. He moves fast.

Page 7 — Summary Questions

1. 1 mark
a dog that is waiting for something

2. 1 mark
Dogs are very loyal animals.

Poetry

1. 1 mark
E.g. Because it shows how excited the dog is.

The Gentleman in Grey

Page 10 — Fact Retrieval Questions

1. 1 mark
in the corner

2. 1 mark each for any of the following answers
2 marks in total
They are shining.
They are black.
They look this way and that.

3. 1 mark each for any of the following answers
3 marks in total
climbs up the shelf
peeps in the mirror
winks at himself
drops from the table
lands with a thump
slides down the sofa
squeaks

4. 1 mark for both correct
candy crumbs
an apple-seed

Page 11 — Inference Questions

1. 1 mark
if you watch it a minute

2. 1 mark
confident

3. 1 mark
E.g. When he comes closer the narrator tells him to "shoo" and "get away".

4. 1 mark
E.g. The gentleman in grey is a mouse.
OR 2 marks
E.g. The gentleman in grey is a mouse — he can make a feast from "the tiniest fragments", so he must be very small.
OR 3 marks
E.g. The gentleman in grey is a mouse — he must be small as he only eats crumbs and is described as "little". The narrator says he has a "velvet hat" which suggests he's soft and furry.

Page 12 — Word Meaning Questions

1. 1 mark
E.g. It moves quietly.

2. 1 mark
E.g. a big meal

3. 1 mark
looks

4. 1 mark
braver

5. 1 mark
thump
AND 1 mark
bump

Page 13 — Summary Questions

1. 1 mark for all correct
The narrator wonders what the gentleman in grey does at night. — 3
The gentleman in grey and his friends eat. — 4
The gentleman in grey arrives. — 2
The gentleman in grey explores the room. — 5
The narrator finds the gentleman in grey and shoos him away. — 6

2. 1 mark
E.g. Mouse in the House

Page 13 — Language Question

1. 1 mark for each appropriate answer
2 marks in total
E.g. They are soft.
They are furry.

Kite Flight

Page 16 — Fact Retrieval Questions

1. 1 mark
on Crocker's Hill

2. 1 mark
There are clouds.

3. 1 mark each for any of the following answers
3 marks in total
greyhound
hawk
gull

4. 1 mark each for any of the following answers
2 marks in total
It crashes onto the ground.
It moves around a bit on the ground.
It stops moving.

Page 17 — Inference Questions

1. 1 mark
E.g. It's a windy day.

2. 1 mark
The kite is flying high up.

3. 1 mark
E.g. The narrator almost has to let go of it.

4. 1 mark
The wind suddenly gets lighter.

Page 18 — Word Meaning Questions

1. 1 mark
flies

2. 1 mark
briefly

3. 1 mark
strength

4. 1 mark
swooping

5. 1 mark
E.g. just touches

Poetry

Page 19 — Language Questions

1. **1 mark for any of the following answers**
   It flies very fast.
   It flies in a straight line.

2. **1 mark**
   E.g. To show that the kite moves awkwardly when it's not in the air, like a fish when it's not in the water.

Page 19 — Structure Questions

1. **1 mark**
   But no, there is a sudden lull;

2. **1 mark**
   E.g. It mentions Crocker's Hill, which is also mentioned in the first verse.

A Night with a Wolf
Page 22 — Fact Retrieval Questions

1. **1 mark for any of the following answers**
   (wild) men
   bears

2. **1 mark**
   under a fir tree by a rock

3. **1 mark**
   They keep each other warm.

4. **1 mark**
   E.g. They leave the hiding place.

Page 23 — Inference Questions

1. **1 mark for any of the following answers**
   There are "wild men" watching.
   There are dangerous animals, such as bears.

2. **1 mark**
   It is "Bending" and "snapping" the pine trees.

3. **a) 1 mark**
   calm
   b) 1 mark
   E.g. He doesn't run away when the wolf comes, but hides with it "Side by side" instead.

4. **1 mark**
   Little one, be not frightened;

Page 24 — Word Meaning Questions

1. **1 mark**
   breaking

2. **1 mark**
   sought

3. **1 mark**
   shone

4. **1 mark**
   E.g. terrible

5. **1 mark**
   beast

Page 25 — Summary Question

1. **1 mark for all correct**
   The narrator and the wolf find the same hiding place. — 3
   The narrator calms the listener's fears. — 4
   The narrator and the wolf help each other. — 5
   The storm arrives. — 2

Page 25 — Prediction Question

1. **1 mark**
   E.g. No, because he got hurt during the storm.
   OR 2 marks
   E.g. Yes, because the narrator had a good experience with the wolf when they helped each other. The narrator says "Little one, be not frightened", which suggests he wasn't scared by what happened.
   OR 3 marks
   E.g. No, because it seemed to be dangerous on the mountain in the bad weather, with trees "Bending" and "snapping". The narrator was hurt in the storm — he was "bruised and blinded". He also had to sleep outside for a whole night.

Out in the Snow
Page 28 — Fact Retrieval Questions

1. **1 mark**
   during the night

2. **1 mark**
   sleigh-bells

3. **1 mark for both correct**
   It is snowy.
   It is sunny.

4. **1 mark for all correct**
   Kate's feather is scarlet. — True
   Bess is dancing. — False
   Joe and Jack are indoors. — False
   Frank and Tom say hallo. — True

Page 29 — Inference Questions

1. **1 mark**
   They want to go out in the snow.

2. **1 mark**
   ice-skating

3. **1 mark**
   E.g. They like the snow.
   OR 2 marks
   E.g. They like the snow. You can tell this because they are laughing.

4. **1 mark**
   E.g. The poem says they grumble about it.
   OR 2 marks
   E.g. The snow makes the graybeards "stumble". This makes them "frown" and grumble.

Page 30 — Word Meaning Questions

1. **1 mark**
   cold

2. **1 mark**
   tingle

Poetry

3. 1 mark
rose

4. 1 mark
E.g. twinkling

Page 31 — Summary Questions

1. 1 mark
Different people's experiences of the snow

2. 1 mark
Young people enjoy the snow.

Page 31 — Structure Question

1. 1 mark
E.g. Both verses mention the snow coming down.

The River's Story

Page 34 — Fact Retrieval Questions

1. 1 mark for any of the following answers
meadows
mountains
woods

2. 1 mark
to drink

3. 1 mark for all correct
damselflies — ballerinas
pike — ambassadors
kingfishers — secret agents

4. 1 mark
bricks

5. 1 mark
behind the derelict housing-estates

Page 35 — Inference Questions

1. 1 mark
E.g. It felt happy.
OR 2 marks
E.g. I think it felt happy, because it says that "life was good".

2. 1 mark
disguised as rainbows

3. 1 mark
E.g. It makes the reader feel sorry for the river.

4. 1 mark
E.g. The factories seem frightening.
OR 2 marks
E.g. The factories seem very large, because they are described as "giants", and they also seem selfish, as their bricks are described as "greedy".
OR 3 marks
E.g. The factories seem frightening, because they left the river "cowering". They have "monstrous shadows", which suggests they are very big. They also seem unpleasant, as the river says they "vomited their poisons" into it.

Page 36 — Word Meaning Questions

1. 1 mark
E.g. fell

2. 1 mark
gossiped

3. 1 mark
wish

4. 1 mark
E.g. blocked

5. 1 mark
E.g. It is very small.

Page 37 — Summary Question

1. 1 mark
River pollution is a bad thing.

Page 37 — Comparison Questions

1. 1 mark
E.g. They have got bigger.

2. 1 mark
E.g. Before the factories grew, the river was clean. After the factories grew, it became dirty and polluted.
OR 2 marks
E.g. Before the factories grew, life was "good" for the river, and lots of animals lived in it or came to it. After the factories grew, the river became polluted.
OR 3 marks
E.g. Before the factories grew, the river flowed through "meadows" and "mountains" and was full of plants and animals. After the factories grew, it became polluted. Instead of plants and animals, it was full of "garbage and junk" and was a "trickle of filth".

0717 - 16220

www.cgpbooks.co.uk